THE BIRTH OF THE NEW TOWN

'Let us boldly enlarge Edinburgh to the utmost.'

('Proposals for carrying on certain public works in the City of Edinburgh', 1752)

This print of 1693 by John Slezer shows the houses of the Old Town huddled beneath the castle

The Georgian House at No. 7 Charlotte Square offers a rare glimpse into the lives of the people who were among the first to move into Edinburgh's late 18th- and early 19th-century New Town, a pioneering architectural project, and the largest of its period anywhere in the world.

The New Town covers about one square mile and contains over 11,000 listed properties, three-quarters of which are still in residential use. Its houses still largely retain their original outer appearance, and the area, together with the city's medieval Old Town, was designated a World Heritage Site in 1995. To fully understand the ambition of this architectural masterpiece, we must first describe the conditions that gave it birth.

'A nation cannot at this day be considerable, unless it be opulent. Wealth is only to be obtained by trade and commerce, and these are only carried on to advantage in populous cities.'

('Proposals' of 1752)

1

Timetable of expansion

Alexander Nasmyth's painting Princes Street with the Commencement of the Building of the Royal Institution, *1825, shows both the medieval Old Town, on the right, and the neo-classical New Town, on the left. The Royal Institution is now the Royal Scottish Academy, at the foot of The Mound*

1752	Publication of the 'Proposals' for the extension of Edinburgh
1753–60	Building of the new Royal Exchange off the High Street (now part of City Chambers)
1759	Draining of the Nor' Loch begun: not completed and replanted until 1820
1765–72	Building of North Bridge, the link between the Old Town and the proposed New Town
1766	Approval of James Craig's plan for the area between Princes Street and Queen Street, St Andrew Square and St George's (later Charlotte) Square
1768	Building of the Theatre Royal (opposite Register House, closed 1859)
1774–88	Building of Register House, designed by Robert Adam and funded from Jacobite estates forfeited to the Crown. Extended 1822–34
1781–3	Construction of The Mound begun: completed in 1830
1787	Opening of the new Assembly Rooms, George Street (financed by public subscription)
1789	Work begun on new university buildings (now known as 'Old College'), designed by Robert Adam (approved in Act of 1785 for South Bridge, and funded by parliament)
1791	Charlotte Square designed by Robert Adam
1806	Completion of the Bank of Scotland building on The Mound
1816	Act of Parliament banning for all time any building on the south side of Princes Street
1820	Completion of Charlotte Square
1822–4	Royal Botanic Garden transplanted from Leith Walk to Inverleith
1824	Completion of the Edinburgh Academy, designed by William Burn
1826	Completion of the Royal Institution (now the Royal Scottish Academy) at the foot of The Mound, designed by William Playfair
1829	Completion of the new Royal High School on Calton Hill, designed by Thomas Hamilton

J M W Turner's watercolour of the Old Town, 1819, vividly conveys its seething life

Edinburgh could truly lay claim to being the capital city of Scotland only after 1535, when the parliament and the College of Justice were set up there. It was then still limited to its 143-acre medieval core – the Old Town – founded in the early 12th century by King David I, and granted a royal charter by Robert the Bruce in 1329. Growing rapidly in the 16th century, but still hemmed in by its protective walls, Edinburgh could only spread upwards rather than outwards. The town became a warren of teeming tenements of up to 11 storeys, where the prosperous occupied the more salubrious middle floors and the poorer people the cellars and the garrets. Often 10 to 12 families lived in the same building, sharing a common stair.

Fire was a constant threat among the close-packed houses, which often had thatched roofs and wooden galleries built over the street: many buildings were lost in the great fires of 1674, 1676 and 1700. Lives were threatened too by the untreated sewage running in the streets – the celebrated cry 'gardy loo' (from the French *gardez l'eau* – beware of the water) warned passers-by below that a chamberpot was about to be emptied from an upstairs window. Lack of light and air among the cramped dwellings also contributed to the prevailing ill-health of the citizens.

This etching, after George Hay, c1814, shows a girl drawing water from a public well in the Old Town, and a caddy

From the late 17th century, water piped from the Pentland Hills allowed the provision of public wells – but it still had to be carried up the steep stairs of the tall tenements by water caddies who charged a penny a cask. These were often elderly women, permanently stooped because of their heavy burdens.

Gladstone's Land

The National Trust for Scotland's property on the Royal Mile is a typical 17th-century Old Town Edinburgh 'land' or tenement building (apartment block). Thomas Gledstanes, a merchant, bought the property on 20 December 1617. He and his family probably occupied an apartment on the third floor and rented out the rest of the building, including two luckenbooths (shops) at street level, to tenants from various backgrounds.

Visitors today can experience a reconstructed merchant's luckenbooth that may have sold cloth and also view the first floor of the tenement which has been furnished by the Trust to give an impression of what a wealthy person's apartment may have looked like in the 17th century. The house retains fine original painted ceiling and wall decoration dating to around 1620, as well as an original Norie painted panel in the Green Room – a Georgian extension. This room has been furnished to reflect the transition in styles from the Old Town to the New Town.

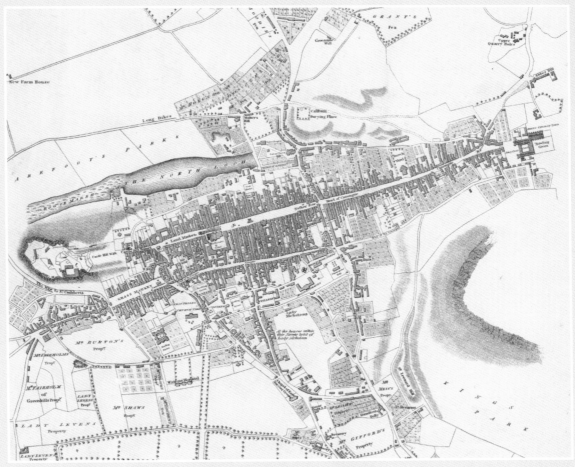

A map of Edinburgh in the 18th century, before its expansion beyond the Old Town

Living conditions became intolerable – by the early 18th century the Old Town was bursting at the seams with around 70,000 inhabitants (there are c11,000 today). In 1753 an Act of Parliament initiated the first of a series of Improvement Acts aimed at alleviating the squalid conditions. The Act provided for a body of trustees, including the Lord Provost, George Drummond, to oversee the improvements. Drummond was the prime mover in the planning of the 'New Town', to be built on the fields of the 'Lang Dykes' to the north of the castle and the insanitary loch that ran beneath it. Already, in 1723, parliament had authorised funds for 'narrowing the noxious lake on the north side of the … City, commonly called the North Loch, into a canal of running water'. Draining of the loch began in 1759, and the Council issued an invitation 'to all gentlemen, farmers, and others, that they are at full liberty to … carry off the dung and fulgie of the North-loch, immediately, and that without payment or other gratuity therefor'. The site remained for many years, according to Lord Cockburn, 'a nearly impassable fetid marsh … the receptacle of many sewers, and seemingly of all the worried cats [and] drowned dogs … of the city'. But the city's march northwards had begun.

> *'The bad situation of Edinburgh has been one great occasion of the poverty and uncleanliness in which the greater part of the people of Scotland live.'*
>
> *(Andrew Fletcher of Saltoun, 1698)*

TRANSFORMING THE CITY

'When we consider the rapid progress which our trade and manufactures have actually made within these few years ... we are persuaded, that an attempt to enlarge and beautify this metropolis, will now at length be deemed necessary.'

('Proposals' of 1752)

Philip Mercier's aquatint of 1782 shows the building of the first New Town, to the left, on its way to completion. The farmland in the foreground is now the site of the Royal Botanic Garden

PROPOSALS
For carrying on certain
PUBLIC WORKS
In the CITY of
EDINBURGH.

AMONG the several causes to which the prosperity of a nation may be ascribed, the situation, conveniency, and beauty of its capital, are surely not the least considerable. A capital where these circumstances happen fortunately to concur, should naturally become the centre of trade and commerce, of learning and the arts, of politeness, and of refinement of every kind. No sooner will the advantages which these necessarily produce, be felt and experienced in the chief city, than they will diffuse themselves through the nation, and universally promote the same spirit of industry and improvement.

Or

The 'Proposals for carrying on certain public works in the City of Edinburgh', published in the Scots Magazine in 1752, took 80 years to carry through and were much inspired by earlier plans of the 1690s and 1720s

George Drummond, a merchant, was born in Perthshire in 1687. He was a leading opponent of the Jacobites, and Lord Provost of Edinburgh for six terms between 1725 and 1764

Edinburgh had lost its status as the capital of a separate kingdom after the union of the Scottish and English crowns in 1603 and the Union of the Parliaments in 1707. But George Drummond, Lord Provost, wanted to promote it as 'the chief city of North Britain', a metropolis fit to compare with London. It needed public buildings – a parliament house, a merchants' exchange, proper accommodation for the supreme courts, a repository for public records, a meeting place for the Town Council, churches, hospitals, and dwellings suitable for the growing professional class, whose work was based in the city. An expanded, enhanced city would also attract the aristocracy who were now beginning to deal in trade and manufacture, and needed town houses as well as country estates.

The Scottish Enlightenment

The visionary 'Proposals' to build the New Town, and their carrying out, would not have been possible without the leap in intellectual curiosity and confidence in the mid-18th century that became known much later as 'the Scottish Enlightenment'. This movement – characterised by Edinburgh advocate Lord Cockburn as 'awakening the intellect, and exciting speculation … the very things that most of the minds … formed a little earlier thought dangerous' – was nurtured by immense economic changes. Trade and commerce had expanded enormously,

John Kay's painting of the 1780s depicts many well-known cultural figures in Edinburgh's Parliament Square. The author Tobias Smollett commented: 'All the people of business in Edinburgh, and even the genteel company may be seen standing in crowds every day, from one to two in the afternoon'

encouraged by the 1707 Act of Union between the Scottish and English parliaments, which in particular opened up the lucrative West Indies trade to Edinburgh's port of Leith. Political conditions for economic growth were favourable, with the relative social peace established in Scotland after the decisive defeat of the Jacobite rebellion at the battle of Culloden in 1746.

The Enlightenment was a Europe-wide movement, characterised by reference to ancient Greek and Roman ideals, and was spurred by rational philosophers on the Continent. But it had its own particular vigour in Scotland, with towering thinkers such as the philosopher and historian David Hume (1711–76), the political economist Adam Smith (1723–90), the pioneering sociologist Adam Ferguson (1723–1816), and a host of others. Edinburgh's debating clubs and forward-thinking publishers such as Archibald Constable spearheaded the intellectual life of the city.

The ferment of ideas permeated the literary, scientific and artistic achievements of the mid-18th to early 19th centuries in Scotland. It nourished artists such as Henry Raeburn and Alexander Nasmyth, and writers such as Walter Scott. In architecture, the spirit of the Enlightenment profoundly influenced Robert Adam, in 1789 the designer of new buildings for the University of Edinburgh, and in 1791 of Charlotte Square.

'A project for enlarging and beautifying this city, could never surely have been suggested at a more proper juncture.'

('Proposals' of 1752)

In 1765 work started on the North Bridge, a vital link between the Old Town and the proposed New Town, as well as to the port of Leith. Its progress was protracted, since the bridge collapsed just after opening to the public in 1769, killing five people, and it had to be redesigned and rebuilt. In 1767 an Act of Parliament – necessary to extend the ancient boundaries of the 'royalty', the original Old Town lands received from the Crown – sanctioned the first building work in the New Town. The Act also allowed for the taxation of inhabitants of the New Town. The construction was to follow the classic gridiron plan of the young architect James Craig, winner in August 1766 of the Town Council's design competition for the project.

The expansion was to be funded by a 'national contribution', to be administered by worthies drawn from the Edinburgh judiciary and the Town Council. Donations towards the project from invited people would be deposited in a bank, and, even as the 'Proposals' were being published, money had begun to flow in. As early as 1716 the Council had bought the area immediately to the north of the Nor' Loch, Bearford's or Barefoots Parks. More land was acquired in the years leading up to 1782, costing the Council around £8,000; the cost of levelling streets, providing drains and laying sewers in the main streets was just under £15,000.

James Craig with his plan for the New Town, by David Allan, c1781

Plots of land in the New Town were sold on a perpetual lease – 'feued' in Scots law terminology – to private individuals or building firms on condition that they adhered to Craig's plan. There were tight prescriptions, for example, on the number and height of storeys in a house. This degree of town planning, though well established in continental Europe, was relatively unknown in Britain: it had been only haphazardly applied in London, though more consistently in Bath.

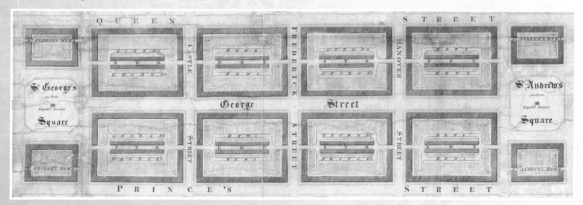

Craig's 'plan of the new streets and squares intended for [the] ancient capital of North Britain', 1767

This striking painting by John Bell is of the Craigleith quarry, to the west of the town. At the height of the building of Craig's New Town, seen in the background, 60 carts made four journeys a day to supply the army of stonemasons on site

Craig's symmetrical design consisted of three principal east-west thoroughfares – George, Queen and Princes Streets (with two lesser streets, Rose Street and Thistle Street, between) linking St Andrew and St George's (later Charlotte) Squares. His plan was to close the design at both ends with symmetrical churches – but Sir Laurence Dundas had already snapped up the feu for the site intended for the St Andrew Square church, and had built for himself the finest mansion in the New Town, now the Royal Bank of Scotland.

The naming of the New Town streets and squares reflected the sense of Edinburgh as the capital of 'North Britain': English symbols such as the rose and St George were combined with Scottish icons like the thistle and St Andrew, in an optimistic evocation of the Union as a forward-looking joint enterprise.

The Mound (or as it was at first known, the Earthen Mound), leading south from the centre of Princes Street, was formed out of earth and rubble displaced by the foundations of houses in the New Town. The Town Council invited builders to lay down their waste here in 1781, with a view to forming a physical link between the Lawnmarket, the main street of the Old Town, and the New Town.

The Bank of Scotland stood at the summit from 1806 (replaced in 1863 by the much modified present version). The site at its foot, now occupied by the National Gallery of Scotland, was traditionally leased by the Council to shows, penny theatres and travelling menageries. In 1819 the Royal Institution for the Encouragement of the Fine Arts was founded and commissioned the building that now houses the Royal Scottish Academy. This was followed in 1850 by the laying of the foundation stone of the National Gallery.

A coloured engraving of The Mound, 1814

This painting of 1843 by Charles Halkerston shows the area at the foot of The Mound still in traditional use for shows and menageries

The striking silhouettes of the neo-classical buildings around The Mound and, beyond, the towering tenements of the Old Town, remain prominent today, largely due to the rejection by successive town councils in the late 18th and early 19th centuries of moves to develop the south side of Princes Street. The area was further enhanced by an Act of 1816, requiring feuars in Princes Street – still at this time largely residential – to fund the laying out of gardens opposite, a feature unique in the main streets of European cities and still one of Edinburgh's prime landmarks.

In 1802, as Craig's design for the first New Town was nearing completion, architects Robert Reid and William Sibbald laid out the second phase to the north of the first, on the steep slope towards the Water of Leith – land owned predominantly by the Heriot's Hospital Trust, commemorated in the name of the first street to be built, Heriot Row (1803–8). This scheme focused on Great King Street, the main east-west axis, terminating to the east in Drummond Place and to the west in Royal Circus (designed by William Playfair in 1820). Further west, the grand Moray Estate, including the 12-sided Moray Place, was completed on an interlinking plan of crescents, ovals and octagons, by James Gillespie Graham, from 1822 to 1830. The painter Sir Henry Raeburn began building on his property at Stockbridge, north of the Water of Leith, around 1813. To the east, William Playfair designed Royal and Regent Terraces, around Calton Hill, after 1820.

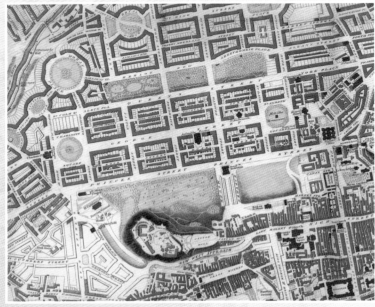

James Kay's plan of 1836 shows the various phases of the New Town completed

Engraving by J H Shepherd of the new Assembly Rooms in George Street, 1829

However, the New Town was not universally admired. Lord Cockburn wrote critically of its uniformity: 'the blunder of long straight lines of street, divided to an inch … by rectangular intersections, every house being an exact duplicate of its neighbour.' He shared a nostalgia for the vivacity of the Old Town with a French visitor, Auguste Blanqui, who commented of the New Town: 'One never sees anyone at the windows of these magnificent palaces, and the doors being constantly shut, could make one think it was a town recently ravaged by an epidemic.'

By 1830 the population of the New Town had grown to around 40,000, living in 5,000 houses. Since 1800, shops had appeared, legal business had begun to be conducted there and the building of the Edinburgh Academy in 1824 provided a classical education for boys. Entertainment was amply catered for at the new Assembly Rooms in George Street, opened in 1787, where charity balls were held regularly, and which also hosted concerts and literary readings. Enthusiasm for playgoing was not quite so widespread – due perhaps to the influence of Presbyterianism – but was popular enough to warrant the building of the Theatre Royal opposite Register House in Shakespeare Square (later Waterloo Place, until recently the site of the main post office). The theatre was opened in 1769, and in the 1780s attracted huge audiences to performances by the famous actress Mrs Sarah Siddons. It was closed in 1859. Register House, designed by Robert Adam as a place to house Scotland's public records and completed in 1788, still stands today.

'Gentlemen's clubs', of which Edinburgh possessed an unusually high number, combined the debating of hot topics with serious drinking sessions. The Friday Club, which met in New Town taverns, was established in 1803 and frequented by distinguished men like Cockburn, Walter Scott, the mathematician John Playfair and the philosopher Dugald Stewart. Entry requirements included a taste for literature and a lack of religious prejudice, and the staple drink was rum punch: 'a very pleasant but somewhat dangerous beverage' commented Cockburn. Ladies, of course, were not admitted to these establishments, where the conversation and the rituals were often very bawdy.

So the wealthier citizens of Edinburgh had less and less need to visit the area they had once inhabited. Deserted by the upper classes, towards the mid-19th century much of the Old Town became one of the worst slums in Europe.

The enormous expenditure on the building of the New Town, visionary though it undeniably was, contributed to the bankruptcy of Edinburgh Town Council in the late 1820s. The unfinished National Monument, 'Edinburgh's Disgrace', begun in 1826 as a memorial to the dead of the Napoleonic Wars but abandoned through lack of funds, still stands on Calton Hill as a stark reminder of this calamity. After 1830, though the professional classes were on the move once more towards the city outskirts, Edinburgh was never again able to afford to expand so rapidly, and on such a scale.

This watercolour by Henry Duguid (fl1828–60) could not depict more graphically the contrast between the dilapidated Old Town and the gleaming New Town, glimpsed like a vision in the distance

The National Monument

The seal of royal approval

The Entry of George IV into Edinburgh from the Calton Hill, 1822, by John Wilson Ewbank

The visit of King George IV to Edinburgh in August 1822 caused huge excitement, confounding initial doubts about how a Hanoverian king would be received in the land of the Stuart challenge to his throne only 80 years earlier. A contemporary Polish diarist, Krystyn Lach-Szyrma, wrote: 'The streets through which he passed were not wide enough, there were not enough roofs or windows to give room to all those anxious to be present.' His arrival at Leith, greeted by spectacular fireworks, and his brief stay were stage-managed down to the last detail by Walter Scott, who had attended the king's coronation the previous year. It was arguably the start of the Romantic (and distorted) notion of Scottishness. Scott had summoned the heads of the clans to give the event a Highland dimension: even those with no connection with the Highlands donned an inauthentic tartan, everyone wore heather in their hats, and George IV himself sported a too-short kilt, famously teamed with flesh-coloured stockings.

Elizabeth Grant of Rothiemurchus reported that there were objections to a man of the king's girth wearing a kilt, but Lady Saltoun tartly retorted: 'Nay, we should take it very kind of him; since his stay will be so short, the more we see of him the better.'

CHARLOTTE SQUARE

'A row of eleven houses composed as a 100-metre palace-front of uncommon finesse and grandeur in which movement is always complemented by stillness, repetition by variety, plainness by intricacy.'

(Edinburgh *in* The Buildings of Scotland *series, by Gifford, McWilliam, Walker and Wilson)*

In 1791 the Council reached agreement with the the Earl of Moray (who owned a crucial portion of the land) to allow the construction of Charlotte Square, the climax of the first section of the New Town. Originally named St George's Square in Craig's plan, it was rechristened to avoid confusion with George Square on the south side of the city. Charlotte was the name of King George III's long-suffering queen.

In response to criticism that the original design had been haphazard, the Council commissioned Robert Adam to design the Square. Adam's vision of the 'palace front', in which the division between individual houses was blurred into a monumental whole, was a completely new departure for architecture in Edinburgh.

As he began work on Charlotte Square, Adam was at the height of his powers – the most celebrated Scottish architect of his day. He was internationally renowned and his influence could be seen throughout Europe and North America. He had been Architect of the King's Works with responsibility for Scotland, and had already designed many buildings in his native country, including Culzean Castle (1777), Mellerstain House (1778) and Newliston House (1789). Adam was paid 200 guineas for his design for the Square, and 5 guineas for a drawing of each individual house.

Robert Adam, son of the famous architect William, was born in Kirkcaldy in 1728. He qualified at Edinburgh University, and then spent several influential years studying in France and Italy

Robert Adam's design for the north and south sides of Charlotte Square, 1791

Adam's superb design – widely acknowledged as a major achievement in European civic architecture of the period – was one of his last, for he was to die from a stomach ulcer only a year later, in March 1792, at his London home. His brother James supervised most of the work after Robert's death, then after James died in 1794 John Paterson, an assistant in the Adam architectural office, took over.

The first feu in the Square, on the north side, was taken in 1792 and the house on that site (No. 6) was very quickly built. Feus on the east and south sides were offered for sale in 1796, and on the west side in 1803. But by 1800 only two-thirds of the north side had been built, and nothing else – the outbreak of the Napoleonic Wars with France, and the widespread fear of invasion, had temporarily put paid to building speculation. Gradually the threat of war receded, and building on the Square recommenced, the south side the last to be completed, in 1820.

Although the Square broadly followed Adam's plan, only the north side, where the Georgian House is situated at No. 7, is almost exactly as he intended. On the other sides, windows were made lower than in the plan, and the amount and shape of the doors differed from Adam's original design. Each side of the Square is 500ft (152m) long. The south side is broadly speaking a replica of the north – both are centred on pediments mounted on four Corinthian pillars, and they have pyramid-shaped roofs – but it lacks the north side's integral 'palace front', as well as striking details such as the guardian sphinxes on the roof. The uses of each floor are signalled by the different finishes of the stone: broached stonework in the basement area, the servants' quarters; rusticated stone base on the ground floor at entrance level; and polished ashlar stone on the upper floors, the families' living quarters.

The greatest deviation from Adam's design was St George's Church: his original plan was not used – perhaps on grounds of expense. In 1810 the Town Council began to raise money for it, from banks and from letting pews, and architect Robert Reid was commissioned to provide a new design. The church, with its conspicuous dome sheathed in copper, was completed in 1814, at a cost of £23,675. The building is now West Register House which, together with the original Register House at the east end of Princes Street, contains the National Archives of Scotland.

Adam's design (1791) and an engraving of 1829 show how much St George's Church had been altered

The Charlotte Square garden

The layout of the garden in the centre of the Square was agreed in March 1797 between the Town Council and the owners of the lots on the north side, under the supervision of William Sibbald, Superintendent of Works to the City. It was derelict wasteland – surrounded by the building site in the Square – until 1803, when it was levelled by the militia of the Inverness-shire Regiment, whose commanding officer, General Alexander Dirom, had a new house at No. 18. However, four years later the garden was still devoid of planting, and residents of the Square successfully appealed to the Town Council for financial help to lay out gravel walks and shrubbery: 'It will greatly tend to improve the appearance of the City if this Square is elegantly fitted up'. The work cost in the region of £1,000.

In 1817 the Square's feuars agreed to an annual charge per household of no more than 2 guineas to maintain the upkeep of the garden. Marjory Fleming remembered that 'the gardens in Charlotte Square were the meeting place of the neighbourhood. From half-past eleven onwards, the children were turned out to play there, unless it was raining'.

By the late 1860s the planting was declining, but the garden took on a new lease of life when the Memorial Committee decided it should be the site of a memorial to Prince Albert, Queen Victoria's beloved consort, who had died in 1861.

During the 19th century some local girls' schools were allowed limited use of the garden. From the 1880s to the 1930s it contained very popular tennis courts. Threats to burrow underneath it to build a railway tunnel or, later, an underground car park, were seen off by the Square's proprietors. Today its primary public use is during the annual Edinburgh International Festival, when it plays host to the Book Festival.

The Albert Memorial, by John Steell. Steell was knighted at the unveiling ceremony in August 1876

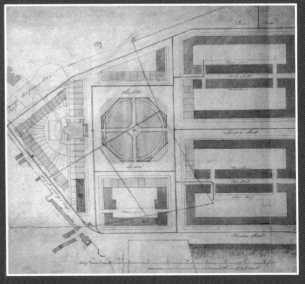

Adam's design for the Square's central garden provided for alternative shapes: the circular version, not Craig's original octagon, prevailed until 1860

A FASHIONABLE ADDRESS: LIVING IN THE SQUARE

Three-fifths of the Square was feued to people who were to live there, rather than to building speculators – lairds, lawyers, doctors, military men and colonial entrepreneurs, who could afford a house second only in prestige to one in St Andrew Square, at the other end of George Street. For many, this was their town house: they also had country residences, sometimes far away in the Highlands, but often in areas we would now think of as part of Edinburgh, for example Bonaly, the site of Lord Cockburn's villa.

Three Charlotte Square dwellers left immensely valuable accounts of their lives here: Elizabeth Grant of Rothiemurchus, author of *Memoirs of a Highland Lady*; Henry Cockburn, who wrote the sharp and engaging *Memorials of his Time*; and Krystyn Lach-Szyrma, a young Polish tutor accompanying the two sons of a Polish prince, who published *Reminiscences of a Journey through England and Scotland 1820–24*.

Elizabeth Grant as a child in the late 1790s, with her mother and sister

An early 19th-century engraving of the north-east corner of Charlotte Square

Elizabeth Grant was born at No. 5 in 1797, one of only three houses then completed in the Square. Her father, a Highland landowner, needed a house in the city in order to pursue his career as a lawyer. 'The French Revolution,' commented Elizabeth, 'in the startling shake it had given to the aristocracy of all Europe … had made it a fashion for all men to provide themselves with some means of earning a future livelihood, should the torrent of democracy reach to other lands.' After an interval spent in London, the family moved back to Charlotte Square in 1817, to 'a house [No. 17] I found the most agreeable of any we had ever lived in in Edinburgh; the shrubbery in front, and the peep from the upper windows at the back, of the Firth of Forth with its wooded shores and distant hills … we were in the midst, too, of our friends … Nothing could be pleasanter than our sociable life'.

The advocate Henry Cockburn, later Lord Cockburn, Solicitor-General for Scotland, lived at No. 14 from 1813 to 1818. He was one of Scotland's noted Whigs (the reformers who were the forerunners of the 19th-century Liberal Party). A frequent guest at dinner parties in the Square, Cockburn recorded in his *Memoirs* that he rarely spent an evening at home alone. Cockburn remembered how he would stand at the corner of Charlotte Square on a summer's evening, when the parkland to the north and west of the Square was still undeveloped, listening to the 'ceaseless rural corn-craiks, nestling happily in the dewy grass'.

A snapshot of some of the other inhabitants of the Square in the late 18th and early 19th centuries gives us a good idea of the social make-up of the neighbourhood.

The feu for No. 6, now the official residence of the First Minister for Scotland, was bought by Orlando Hart, a shoemaker, who had a house built to Adam's specifications and sold it in 1797 to Mrs Isabella Crauford, widow of a banker and Jamaica plantation owner. In 1806 it was acquired by Sir John Sinclair, 1st Baronet of Ulbster in Caithness and editor of the *First Statistical Account of Scotland*.

Portrait of Lord Cockburn by Sir John Watson Gordon

At Nos. 2 and 18 respectively were two military men: Colonel Alexander Baillie and General Alexander Dirom, Quartermaster-General in Scotland. A military supplies contractor, Sir William Fettes of Wamphray, moved into No. 13 in 1807: he was Lord Provost of Edinburgh in 1800 and 1804, and Fettes Academy is named after him. Two men who had made money in India, James Hay and then James Paton, lived at No. 8: they were followed by banker William Ramsay, whose cellars boasted '219 dozen port wine, 12 dozen claret, 10 bottles champagne, 7 galls whisky in bottles'. Another banker, Sir John Marjoribanks of Lees, occupied No. 12, where, in January 1814, he organised a reception for a hundred guests to honour the writer Walter Scott with the Freedom of the City. The Earl of Glasgow lived at No. 31. Robert Reid, the architect who designed St George's Church in the Square, clearly liked it here, for he lived at No. 44.

THE GEORGIAN OWNERS OF NO. 7

A copy of the portrait of John Lamont, by Henry Raeburn

Above: Catherine Farquharson, by Sir John Watson Gordon
Opposite: The charter of sale to John Lamont of No. 7 Charlotte Square

John Lamont bought No. 7 in 1796 for £1,800 (around £1.6m in today's money) from the builder-architect Edmund Butterworth, who had snapped up several feus in the Square. The Lamonts lived at 69 Princes Street (roughly the site of the BHS shop today) while the house was completed. The eldest of seven children, Lamont was born about 1741. He became the 18th Chief of the Clan Lamont in 1767 and inherited the Ardlamont estate in Argyll, deriving income from rent from his tenants. In 1773 he married Helen Campbell and the couple had five children – John, Amelia, Georgina, Norman and Helen Elizabeth. Amelia married Duncan Campbell of Ross the year after the family moved into No. 7.

John Lamont inherited some debts, but his extravagant lifestyle, including extended stays in London, where he was involved in Whig politics, worsened his financial problems. His son Norman also incurred debts, adding to the family's plight. In 1809 Lamont sold one of his Highland estates for over £40,000, and in 1815 chose to sell No. 7 too, for £3,000. He died the following year at Ardlamont, still heavily in debt.

No. 7 was bought by Catherine Farquharson of Invercauld, who also rented the Lamonts' furniture for £50 a year. Catherine was a 41-year-old widow with three children; her husband, a Royal Navy captain, had died in 1809. Her father had died in the same year and, as the only survivor of eleven children, Catherine inherited the family property near Braemar. The 1841 census shows that she kept eight servants at Charlotte Square and that an elderly relative also stayed in the house. Catherine lived here until her death in 1845 at the age of 70.

Our exploration of the Georgian House focuses on the life of its inhabitants during this period.

Charter

In Favours of

John Lamont Esqr

To All and Sundry

[wh]om these presents may Concern We The Right Honble
[Si]r James Stirling Baronet Lord Provost of the
[Cit]y of Edinburgh, David Milne James Eyre,
[Da]vid Hunter and George Spankie Esqrs Bailies
[ther]eof Neil Macvicar Esqr Dean of Guild and
[Pa]trick Crichton Esquire Treasurer of the same
[a]nd also the remanent Members of Council all
representing the Community of the said City
Proprietors of the Lots or Area hereafter
[m]entioned Whereas by Articles and Conditions of Roup
[of] Nine Lots or Areas for building on the Northside of
[Char]lotte Square dated the Twenty Eight day of March
[an]d Recorded in the Borough Court Books of Edinr
[the] Seventeenth day of April One thousand seven
[hu]ndred & Ninety two And subscribed by The
[Ri]ght Honble Sir James Stirling present Lord

LIFE IN THE GEORGIAN HOUSE

ABOVE STAIRS

THE LOBBY AND INNER HALL

Guests were received in the entrance hall by servants, dismounting from their carriage or sedan chair with the aid of the built-up sections of kerb that you can still see all around Charlotte Square. Many of the front steps in the Square retain their original iron boot-scrapers and inverted trumpets built into the iron railings, where the 'link boys' who accompanied the guests with a lighted torch could extinguish it.

Lobbies were very practically furnished, with wooden-seated hall chairs where servants could wait, a table for visitors' cards, and hat and greatcoat stands. There is evidence that this draughty area was originally warmed by a stove set into the west wall, on the left as you enter. The stone floor is characteristic of houses of the Georgian period, and the glazed screen is a replacement by the National Trust for Scotland – many houses had these draught-excluding doors. The delicate stone-coloured paint resembles the colour that was originally used in the hall.

The mahogany stick barometer in the inner hall was made around 1800 by Lenone of Calton Street, Edinburgh. The regulator, a precision timepiece that did not strike, was made by David Ross in Dingwall in the late 18th century. The pineapple doorstop reflects a common motif in wrought iron decoration throughout the New Town.

John Kay's etching shows the sedan chair 'taxi' service provided by chairmen, often Highlanders, who waited for custom on the corners of New Town streets. Only the very wealthy could afford their own chairs

THE STAIRCASE

In the evening, guests were taken up to the drawing room on the first floor as soon as they arrived, to be greeted by their host and hostess. The stairs had to be well lit, with the lamps hanging from wrought iron brackets: gas lighting was not installed until around 1820, and electricity a century later. During the day, the staircase was illuminated by the oval dome (cupola) at the top of the house. The interior stone staircases of New Town houses were a contrast to the cramped wooden stairs of Old Town dwellings. More expensive to build, they were also more durable, fire-resistant and easier to keep clean.

THE DRAWING ROOM

The drawing room was used to display the family's wealth and possessions. To shield the south-facing room and its contents from harmful sunlight, the wooden blinds would be closed during the day, unless a group of ladies was meeting here for tea or cards. Dustcovers were used to protect the furniture and were removed when the family were entertaining guests in the evening.

Harden's sketch of evening entertainment in late Georgian Edinburgh. Young people were expected to learn social accomplishments such as playing the piano, singing and dancing. For women, showing these skills at social gatherings was vital to prove that they would make good wives – without a husband their economic futures would be very insecure

This room was considered to be the most impressive in the house and was used for formal evening entertaining: after gathering here, guests would proceed with elaborate formality downstairs again for dinner. Lach-Szyrma recorded: 'When dinner is announced, the hostess asks for the arm of the guest whom she wishes to honour most, and everybody else follows in pairs … One cannot offer one's arm to or address a lady to whom one has not been introduced.'

The drawing room was also where entertainment continued after dinner, first for the ladies, who returned here while the gentlemen remained in the dining room smoking and drinking port and brandy. Lach-Szyrma wrote: 'When the glasses have been filled several times and the conversation becomes more lively and free, the hostess gives a sign to the ladies to retire … An hour or an hour and a half after the ladies have left, the hostess sends word that tea is ready. The gentlemen then join the ladies and immediately their gaiety changes into respectful gravity.' In contrast, Elizabeth Grant tartly commented: 'Gentlemen seldom reappeared in the drawing-room after dinner, [and] they made, as the wine merchant thought, excellent use of their freedom from ladies' society.'

Here, the ladies played the piano or sang, many guests played cards, backgammon or chess, and the company would not disperse until after midnight, later if there was a dance, which was followed by a cold supper. Although public balls were held weekly at the Assembly Rooms in George Street, in aid of charity, private dances became increasingly popular. Elizabeth Grant observed that, by 1817, 'a much more pleasant style of smaller parties had come into fashion with the new style of dancing. It was the first season of quadrilles …Two, or at most three, instruments sufficed for band, refreshments suited better than suppers'. Drawing rooms like this one contained little enough furniture for it to be moved easily to the side of the room, to allow the dancing to begin.

A typical Robert Adam plaster frieze and cornice have been restored. The green colour is based on the Trust's research into paint schemes at Culzean Castle, also designed by Adam, and being built at the same time as Charlotte Square.

The seat furniture, which dates from 1785–90, came as a bequest from Yester House, East Lothian, and has been covered in the striped watered silk that became fashionable before the Regency period with which it is so associated. The carpet was specially woven by Brintons of Kidderminster in 2011, and follows a design of 1797 from their pattern archives.

By the fireplace is a petit point firescreen, designed to protect visitors' faces from the intense heat of the coal fire. The Derby china pastille burners on the mantelpiece heated scented oils, which disguised the body odours that would have been more evident then than now, since regular bathing was much less easy.

The beauty of the room was enhanced at night by the light reflected from the cut-glass chandelier and from the candles placed in front of the mirrors, or pier glasses, between the windows. Guests would have been impressed by the lighting, since the chandelier required 12 candles and the sconces another 12: the candles were made of beeswax, which was taxed and therefore very expensive.

The square piano

An essential component of a room dedicated to entertaining, this mahogany-case piano was made by Edinburgh cabinetmaker Richard Horsburgh (one of three or four people making musical instruments in Edinburgh at this time) in 1802. There are no sustaining pedals and it has only five octaves: modern pianos have eight, in a longer keyboard. Significantly, this piano has its original strings. Very few of Horsburgh's instruments still survive, even though Edinburgh was the most important musical centre in Scotland: the flourishing Edinburgh Musical Society promoted the making of instruments as well as the performance of music. Square pianos remained popular in Scotland much longer than in England, where the grand piano was becoming more fashionable. The sheet music on the piano – sonatas and selected Scottish airs – was composed by John Ross of Aberdeen. The flute, of about the same date as the piano, is made of boxwood with silver and ivory mounts.

The height of fashion

Two children, their mother and a maid in a New Town drawing room, as sketched by John Harden in 1810. His collection of drawings is the only known contemporary representation of life in New Town interiors of the Georgian period

The ample drawing room, occupying the whole width of the house, was the ideal space for women to promenade and show off their outfits. During the Georgian period, the wide skirts and huge hair of the earlier 18th century gave way to the simpler, narrower silhouette of the 'Empire line', inspired by Greek and Roman antiquity, with a high waist, floating shawls and hair bound up simply with ribbon in the classical style.

But, as Elizabeth Grant recorded, there was still room for extravagance. A whalebone-based corset would be covered by a dress of silk, 'and then with lace or net, and hung about with festoons of lace and beads, garlands of flowers, puffings of ribbon, furbelows of all sorts. As the waists were short, how the imprisoned victims managed their arms we … can hardly imagine'. Lord Cockburn observed that the aristocracy of both sexes clung to elaborate powdered hair arrangements, 'while the discontented exhibited themselves ostentatiously', aping the fashions of the French revolutionaries, 'in all the Jacobinism of clean natural locks'.

THE PARLOUR

Guests for afternoon tea or for an informal gathering were shown into the Parlour, at the back of the house on the first floor.

The family also relaxed here, reading books or newspapers. Edinburgh was a highly literate and politically engaged society, and the talk in this room would reflect that. *The Scotsman* was first published in Edinburgh in January 1817 and quickly gained a wide circulation as a well-regarded voice of opposition to the Tory government. Here, also, letters would be written. The women did needlework, embroidering designs like that on the firescreen, and paperwork, such as the 'quilling' on the tea caddy on the central table, made up of tiny spirals of rolled-up paper. The early 19th-century barrel organ between the windows provided a musical background to these pastimes.

Children spent some time in here with their parents, often being taught by their mother. But they were usually confined to the nursery (which no longer exists in this form in the Georgian House) on the third floor. Boys had tutors or attended the Royal High School (first in the Old Town, then on Calton Hill), and from 1824 the Edinburgh Academy (in the New Town). They went to university for a general education at the early age of 12 or 13, specialising later in law, medicine, theology and other professional subjects. Girls remained at home, learning domestic skills.

The pair of globes in this room – one terrestrial, the other celestial – were made around 1810 by Cary, considered to be the finest globemakers of the Georgian period. The globes were used in the education of the children of the house and would be kept up to date by pasting new maps on top of the old

The art of tea

Tea – then a recent import from China – was a fashionable drink in the Georgian period. Its serving was accompanied by elaborate ritual and elegant accessories such as the mahogany tea-table in the Parlour, with its three hinged and tin-lined compartments for green tea, black tea and sugar, and the tea caddies near the fireplace. Tea was taxed and therefore expensive, so the lady of the house kept the keys to prevent the servants from helping themselves (they were permitted to use the spent tea leaves).

The pretty tea service on the breakfast table in the Parlour is Minton china, and was made around 1810.

THE DINING ROOM

Both Lord Cockburn and Lach-Szyrma documented the gradual postponement of 'dinner', in the course of the late 18th and early 19th centuries, from 2pm to 6pm. This reflected the growing influence of the business-oriented middle classes, who preferred to eat at the close of their working day.

Lach-Szyrma observed a typical New Town dinner with close attention: 'The dining-room tables are generally oblong, covered with snowy linen … The light of the crystal chandeliers reflects itself in the crystal and silver.' Once the guests were seated, with the host at the sideboard end of the table, the meal began. 'Dinner consists of three courses. The first dishes are already on the table when the guests arrive and, when everybody is seated, the menservants take off the covers. There are one or two kinds of soup, fish, fowl, ham, beef and roast mutton and, for vegetables, cabbage, spinach and potatoes. The soup is ladled out by the hostess, the fish and meat carved by the host and the servants hand it round. Other dishes are dealt out by the person in front of whom they happen to be placed. To do this well one should have some practice … The second course consists of game, fowls, pies, cheeses, sweets, cakes, jam and puddings. … The third course is dessert. Apples, pears, nuts, figs, dates, almonds, raisins and oranges are all left on the table in great profusion till the end of dinner.'

Towards the end of the first course, drinks were handed round: port, ale, Madeira, sherry, claret, and in wealthy households burgundy, Rhine wine and champagne. The 'dumb waiters' at both ends of the sideboard supplemented the service given by the servants of the house, allowing the hosts and guests to serve themselves during private conversations. All the plates, glasses and cutlery for the meal were laid out on the sideboard, so it was well lit with candles – here in two vestal-virgin holders, one an original from the Georgian New Town. Less elegantly to modern eyes, the sideboard also holds a pewter chamberpot that the gentlemen would use once the ladies had retired from the room.

The dinner service here is Wedgwood and the pattern dates to 1812; the rest is in the china closet in the basement. Most of the 'silver' is actually Old Sheffield plate (copper, with silver plating on top), dating from 1785–1805 – very popular with the professional class, since it was much cheaper than the solid silver traditionally favoured by the aristocracy. The table knives have broad, flat scimitar-shaped blades – unlike today, it was acceptable to eat from a knife.

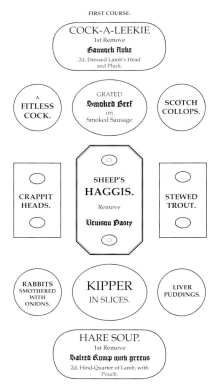

FIRST COURSE.

COCK-A-LEEKIE
1st Remove
Bannock Fluke
2d, Dressed Lamb's Head and Pluck.

A FITLESS COCK.

GRATED Smoked Beef on Smoked Sausage

SCOTCH COLLOPS.

CRAPPIT HEADS.

SHEEP'S HAGGIS.
Remove
Venison Pasty

STEWED TROUT.

RABBITS SMOTHERED WITH ONIONS.

KIPPER IN SLICES.

LIVER PUDDINGS.

HARE SOUP.
1st Remove
Salted Rump with greens
2d, Hind-Quarter of Lamb, with Pouch.

This 1826 table setting for 'a St Andrew's Day or Burns Club dinner' shows the variety of food a diner would expect

If the Lamonts had overnight guests, they would also take breakfast in this room – at no set time. It could include porridge and cream, Finnan haddock and poached eggs, baps, scones or oatcakes with butter, honey or marmalade.

The original black marble chimneypiece was a traditional feature of dining rooms of this period. The colour scheme has been reproduced as it was in 1796, the year the house was built. The floor is original, with broad oak boards, and the walls show the original pine panelling, grained to resemble mahogany. The room also still features the original plain plaster cornice. The deep bay windows are due to Adam's design of the external pilasters on bases. The writing desk, dating from c1800, is here because this room was used for doing business as well as for dining – without guests, there was often only one fire lit in the house, in the dining room.

Most of the houses on this side of Charlotte Square were planned with dining rooms to the rear on the ground floor, benefiting from the open views to the sea across Lord Moray's pleasure grounds, which were later developed to create Moray Place. These north side houses are less sophisticated in their planning, allowing for a variety of room uses, than the highly specialised plans of later New Town houses like those of Moray Place.

The Georgian supermarket

The ingredients for these lavish New Town dinners would have been bought at the food market under the North Bridge, which was patronised by both the rich and poor, and sold everything. Fresh fish was brought from the sea at dawn by fisherwomen, laden with full creels on their backs: a herring or a crab could be had for a penny, a lobster for threepence. Beef, veal, mutton, fowl and game of all kinds were available here, together with a range of vegetables that we would consider quite sophisticated today, including spinach, asparagus, artichokes, broccoli, endive and a variety of herbs. In contrast to our supermarket produce, available everywhere and all year round, food was local and seasonal – strawberries, cherries, gooseberries, apples, pears, peaches, quinces, figs and grapes (but no oranges) marked the different months of the year. There was no refrigeration to keep food fresh, so it would be bought daily.

Shepherd's engraving of the North Bridge and the food market underneath

THE NECESSARY PASSAGE

There was no bathroom in the house in the Georgian period, so between the Dining Room and the Bedchamber is a portable water closet, dating from 1805 and made in London by Blades & Palmer of Piccadilly (1803–22), and still bearing its maker's instructions. The brass handle operated the flush from the hand-filled water tank at the back, discharging the contents of the pan into a copper basin below, which would be emptied by a housemaid. Strips of newspaper and straw served as toilet paper. Scavengers employed by the Town Council collected the household waste, including excrement, every day. Late 19th-century plans show that a toilet had been installed on the ground floor and a bathroom on the first floor, connected to mains water supply, drainage and sewers.

Although Edinburgh Town Council had dispatched the New Town's designer, James Craig, to London to learn what he could about sewer building, it could only afford to install them in the main streets. Often they were not laid until houses had been occupied for several years. Meanwhile the Council made money by selling the New Town's 'dung' as fertiliser to gentleman farmers outside the city! The Town Council laid on the New Town's water supply, but individual feuars paid for the installation of a water pipe into their own buildings.

In 1819 the growing need for water in the expanding New Town led to the setting up of the Edinburgh Joint Stock Water Company, which commissioned Thomas Telford to design a gravity feed system bringing water in cast-iron pipes from the Glencorse Valley in Midlothian to Queen Street. No. 7 had gained its water supply by this time, with the installation of a pump in the scullery.

Georgian artists

Three of the best known artists of the Georgian period, all leading figures in the Scottish Enlightenment and working for most of their lives in Edinburgh, are represented in the fine collection of paintings in this house.

Allan Ramsay (1713–84) established a substantial clientele early in his career as a portraitist in Edinburgh, with the help of introductions by his father, the well-known poet Allan Ramsay. But his style developed dramatically after visiting Italy, and he became famous for his ability to depict the individuality rather than simply the status of his sitters, pioneering a new direction in 18th-century British art. In 1767 Ramsay was appointed Principal Painter in Ordinary to King George III. Also an essayist and a friend of Voltaire, Rousseau, Hume, Adam Smith and Robert Adam, Ramsay was a celebrated British cultural figure of this period and is now regarded as one of its foremost artists. His *Portrait of an Unknown Lady*, displaying his mastery in painting textures, hangs in the Drawing Room.

A Portrait of an Unknown Lady

St Bernard's Well and the Water of Leith, Edinburgh

Alexander Nasmyth (1758–1840) also began his career as a portrait painter, having studied under Allan Ramsay in London. You can see in the Parlour his portrait of Jane Ross of Shandwick, who inherited her uncle's Edinburgh estate (remembered in the name Shandwick Place, just round the corner from Charlotte Square) and died there in a fire in 1829. A trip to Italy and a close friendship with Robert Burns developed Nasmyth's interest in landscape painting, a genre in which he excelled and whose development he greatly influenced. His painting of St Bernard's Well in the Drawing Room – which seems bathed in an Italian rather than a Scottish light – depicts a structure of his own design (which still survives), built to surround a natural spring beside the Water of Leith, thought to possess healing properties. It is based on a classical temple at Tivoli, near Rome, and shelters a statue of Hygeia, the Greek goddess of health.

Sir Henry Raeburn (1756–1823), who lived nearby in the then village of Stockbridge, was one of the finest Scottish portraitists of his day, unique in his ability to capture the character of his sitter. He was much in demand, and was commissioned by John Lamont to paint his portrait, a reproduction of which is on display above the door to the Bedchamber. Dominating the Dining Room is Raeburn's imposing full-length portrait of Alexander Keith of Ravelston and Dunottar (on loan to the Trust), presented in a rustic Scottish landscape. Keith was a pillar of contemporary Edinburgh society, and he left £1,000 in his will for the promotion of science. He was a good friend of Sir Walter Scott, who wryly described him as 'a most excellent man, but the most irresolute in the world … especially when the question was unloosing his purse-strings'. The portrait has a connection with this house, since Keith's nephew and heir Alexander married John Lamont's daughter Georgina in September 1813.

Alexander Keith of Ravelston and Dunottar

THE BEDCHAMBER

Early New Town houses were very flexible in their layout, and it was common to find the main bedroom on the ground floor in this period. In the 19th century this room may have been used as a dining room; it originally contained a sideboard recess, like the Dining Room, indicating that both rooms were used for large dinner parties. Even as a bedroom, this space was never exclusively intended for sleeping: Mrs Lamont would have used it as a sitting room, for pursuing her hobbies and for receiving female visitors in the morning. The mid-18th-century boudoir spinning wheel was seen as a sign of virtue at this time.

A fine four-post bed like this would have been shown off to guests, who were encouraged to enter what we would now regard as a very private space. The National Trust for Scotland was fortunate to receive the loan of this splendid bed from Newliston, a country house in West Lothian owned at this time by Thomas Hog and also designed by Robert Adam. The late 18th-century bed still has most of its original hangings which were appliquéd by Lady Mary Hog in 1774. When the bed was first offered to the Trust, the hangings were grey as a result of years of shale mining pollution in the area. Careful washing restored them to their original colour. The original bedspread (made from two of the hangings) is now in store, and this one was quilted and hand-stitched in Glasgow in the late 18th century using Indian cotton imported via the East India Company.

The pouches on the bed-head are to hold pocket watches: they kept the sensitive workings insulated from the cold and in an upright position (a watch lying flat overnight could lose up to one-and-a-half hours). Designed by Lady Mary herself, they are a very rare feature on beds of this period.

The washing facilities in the Bedchamber – a washstand for the hands and face and a bidet – were commonly seen in households at this time.

Home remedies

The mahogany-cased travelling dispensary in the bedchamber was made by James Robertson & Co. of George Street, Edinburgh, in 1830. It still contains 22 of the original 29 bottles, along with measuring scales, a glass pestle and mortar for mixing ingredients, and two porcelain spoons. Most wealthy households would own a medicine chest, to which the lady of the house kept the keys. She would treat the family when they fell ill, thereby avoiding costly visits from the doctor. One of the medicines in this chest, laudanum, was widely taken as a painkiller: it is a derivative of opium and is now regarded in Britain as a Class A drug. Another, chloroform, was used as an expectorant in cough mixtures – its anaesthetic properties were not discovered until 1847.

Gregory's Mixture, a remedy for stomach upsets consisting of magnesia, powdered rhubarb and ginger, was popular well into the 20th century. It was developed in 1790 by James Gregory, Professor of Medicine at Edinburgh University. Many other remedies in the chest are still familiar: castor oil and Epsom salts as laxatives; peppermint and calcium carbonate (labelled 'prepared chalk') for indigestion; clove essence for toothache; camphor for colds; and calamine for inflammation. Others, such as those containing mercury, are now known to be dangerous.

Until the early 19th century smallpox was the most fatal childhood disease: it was subsequently greatly diminished by vaccination, first used in 1796 by the pioneering English medical scientist Edward Jenner. However, there were measles epidemics in Edinburgh in 1806–7 and 1816–17, and whooping cough, diphtheria and tuberculosis also continued to take their toll throughout the 19th century, particularly among the poor in the Old Town, whose diet and insanitary living conditions gave them little resistance to disease, and whose access to medical help was dependent on charity.

A view of the garden

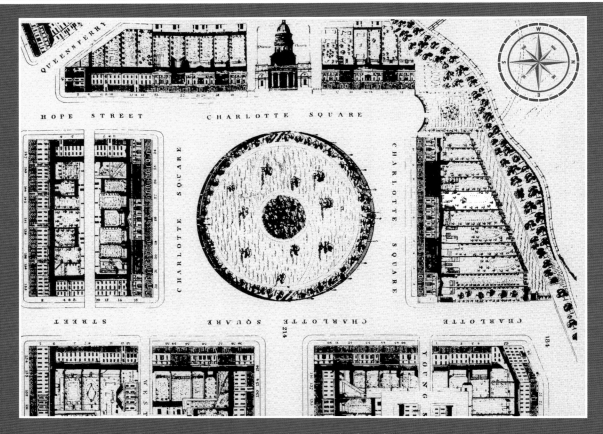

Robert Kirkwood's map of 1819 shows all 11 gardens on the north side of Charlotte Square, each with its own design. From the back of No. 7 a curving path leads past shrubs to join an oval walk that extends almost to the end of the garden

In the Lamonts' day, one of the delights of the rooms at the back of the house would have been the view over the garden and beyond, to the parkland sloping down to the Water of Leith, to the ships plying to and fro on the Firth of Forth and to the distant hills of Fife. James Craig's 1767 plan shows a coach-house and stable mews beyond the garden, but although these were built for other houses in the Square, they were not provided here, perhaps because of restrictions imposed by the neighbouring Moray estate. John Lamont's mews were in Young Street Lane, just off Charlotte Square.

For families who had lived in the cramped Old Town, a private garden would have been a particular pleasure: they could stroll here and supervise their children playing. One of Elizabeth Grant's only memories of her infancy at No. 5 was 'a certain waggon full of black sacks which represented coals, which I vainly attempted to pull or push up some steps in the garden'. The garden may also have acted as a drying green for washing and a 'bleaching green' for household linen.

Seed catalogues of the Georgian era demonstrate that many of the plants we enjoy today were also popular then, including asters, dahlias, delphiniums, irises, lilies, phlox, violas and primulas, as well as vegetables and fruit trees. They were widely available from market gardens and nurseries all around Edinburgh.

BELOW STAIRS

John Harden's drawing shows servants busy in the wine cellar

The lifestyle of the Lamonts depended on a team of servants, and the basement of No. 7 was their domain. Up to 11 servants were employed by one householder in Charlotte Square – at No. 7 there were between 5 and 7. A manservant could earn up to £40 a year, but a maidservant only £8–£12. Many lived in the Old Town, or in the mews lodgings of the New Town. Those who lived on the premises were kept out of sight: 'If there is a third floor', recorded Lach-Szyrma, 'it is generally designed for garrets or for servants' bedrooms. But as a rule these live in the basements where the kitchen is also to be found ... the servants go through [a little gate] to their basements, while the masters have another entrance.'

Servants often came from rural areas, where poverty and the Highland Clearances forced thousands to flood into Edinburgh and Glasgow. Living standards for the poor had improved in the late 18th century, but much less than for the rich. Lord Cockburn recorded that in March 1795 11,000 people – one-eighth of the population of Edinburgh – were fed by charity. The staple diet for the poor was oatmeal, milk, potatoes, carrots and fish where available locally. Domestic servants were fed well, clothed, and given accommodation if their families did not live nearby.

The wine cellar

The servants of No. 7 Charlotte Square worked very long hours – often as many as 112 hours a week for a maid – and were at the beck and call of the family. They could be summoned via the bell pulls in every room, to attend to fires, fetch hot water for tea and for washing, and a host of other tasks. When the house was first occupied, water was not piped in but was supplied by water caddies charging a penny a barrel from the public well. Once running water had been laid on, it could be drawn from the pump in the scullery. Servants had to be strong to carry it up many stairs – and to carry food and crockery from the kitchen up to the dining room (a bucket loaded with six plates weighed six kilos).

The spiral springs on this bellboard are notably a Scottish feature, instead of the customary English 'question marks'

A time of repression

The poor had very few means of improving their lot, and they did not have the vote. Repression rather than social reform was the order of the day, stimulated by the government's mortal fear of a revolutionary upsurge of the kind that had occurred in France in 1789. During the following decade in Scotland, a first conviction for 'sedition' – in other words, opposition to the government – was punishable by transportation to the colonies, and even execution. In 1794, Thomas Muir, the famous radical advocate and political agitator, was condemned in Edinburgh to 14 years' hard labour in Botany Bay – a sentence that shocked even the conservative establishment. Despite the prospect of harsh punishment, the notorious Edinburgh 'mob' frequently sought redress in the only way open to them – the pelting of detested politicians with dead cats was not uncommon.

Throughout this period civilian militias were constantly mobilised in Edinburgh to deal with popular unrest, as well as with the threat of invasion from France: Sir Walter Scott enjoyed organising and drilling these volunteers. In 1820 the organised movement of the radical weavers in Glasgow provoked perhaps the greatest panic yet experienced by Edinburgh's gentry. Public executions, sometimes of women, for petty crimes, that took place regularly in the Old Town's Grassmarket, are perhaps the strongest reminder of the brutal underside of Edinburgh's gracious Georgian society.

A public execution in Edinburgh's Grassmarket: engraving by James Skene of Rubislaw (1775–1864)

The men and women who ran the house

A hierarchy as strict as that of their employers governed the servants' lives, and each of them had very specific tasks. First in line of superiority was the butler, a general manservant, whose duties included those of footman and valet. He supervised the other servants and hired additional ones when required for a particularly large dinner party. The butler monitored the supply of wine and ale, held the key to the wine cellar and chose which wine to serve with meals. As footman he cleaned the cutlery, Sheffield plate and shoes. As well as waiting at table, he would be expected to answer the door and run errands. As valet, he helped his master wash, shave and dress, and kept his clothes clean. The butler slept in the basement, probably in what is now the shop: it had the luxury of a fireplace.

Next in importance was the housekeeper, if the family was wealthy enough to employ one, who kept accounts and paid tradesmen's bills, which she then settled with her mistress. If there was no housekeeper, these duties fell to the cook, who also had the responsibility of buying and preparing the family's food, and so earned more than any other female servant. She was expected to run the kitchen as economically as possible. Her room was probably opposite the kitchen (now the utility room). The cook was helped in the kitchen by the kitchen or scullery maid, the youngest and lowest-paid servant despite being the most hard-worked. Often in her first job and as young as ten or eleven, she would be up very early to light the kitchen fire and heat water for cooking and washing. She prepared food under the cook's direction, and had to keep the kitchen, scullery, larder and all utensils clean.

Pencil drawing of a servant girl by Edinburgh artist Walter Geikie (1795–1837)

The housemaid(s) made and repaired all the household linen, cleaned the furniture, floors and the fireplaces, laid and lit the coal fires and made the beds. They would open and close the shutters, fetch water for the family to wash, and to them fell the unenviable task of emptying the chamberpots. Because they had to do many jobs before the family awoke, they rose about 5am. In what is now the touch-screen room was a servants' bedroom: there are no windows, so meagre ventilation was provided by the shutters at the top of the door. The present-day film room was probably the servants' sitting room, since it has a small fireplace: some of the servants would have slept here, too, on fold-up beds.

Nurserymaids looked after the children, washing and dressing them, mending their clothes and serving their meals. They slept in the attic rooms on the third floor of the house, where the nursery once was.

41

THE KITCHEN

This room was the hub of the basement: hot, smoky and a constant hive of activity. During restoration work, evidence of no fewer than four ovens was found, including an open fire range and a separate baking oven. The range, the focal point of the area, was used for all boiling, roasting and grilling: a fan fitted in the chimney rotated in the upward draught of hot air, providing power to turn the spit. This early 19th-century range was rescued in the 1970s from a skip in nearby India Street. The hot plate to the left of the range supplemented the main range when a large meal was being prepared. The charcoal grate was placed under the window to allow the fumes to escape: it was made by W & P Steele in Edinburgh and, like the bed upstairs, came from Newliston House, West Lothian.

The gleaming copper pans – there are no fewer than 20, all different sizes – were cleaned with vinegar or lemon skins dipped in salt and silver sand. They are lined with tin to prevent the formation of verdigris, which is highly poisonous. Even empty, the pans were very heavy for the cook and the kitchen maid to lift.

In the late 18th and early 19th centuries, sugar cones like the one on the table were a familiar sight. Raw sugar was imported chiefly from the West Indies and refined in Britain, but the process of granulating sugar was not invented until 1837. In the Lamonts' day, pieces would be cut off the cone using the sugar cutters on the dresser and the nippers on the table: it could then be ground in the pestle and mortar.

Traces of the original blue wall paint were found under many coats of whitewash: many kitchens of this period were painted this colour, as it was commonly thought to deter flies.

Only the lady of the house, or the housekeeper, would hold the key to the china closet, which housed the family's precious china. The items here are based on an 1826 inventory relating to a New Town house in Heriot Row. They include the rest of the Wedgwood dinner service and the Minton tea service displayed upstairs; two Derby chamberpots of 1780 featuring both an English rose and a Scottish thistle; and a large chest for the transport of silverware.

THE OWNERS OF NO. 7 AFTER THE GEORGIAN PERIOD

In 1845 Lord Charles Neaves, a distinguished criminal lawyer, bought No. 7. He was Solicitor-General for Scotland (1852–3) and in 1853 succeeded his neighbour Lord Cockburn on the Bench (was made a judge). Five years later Neaves was appointed a Lord of Justiciary. Known for his sociability, he also wrote 'lively, witty and sarcastic' verse. The 1851 census reveals that Neaves and his wife Elizabeth had eight children and six servants. Ten years later there were ten children still at home and – doubtless reflecting Neaves's increased income as a judge – ten servants, including a butler and a pageboy. The 1881 census shows that Elizabeth was now a widow, with only her three unmarried daughters living with her; however, they still employed seven servants.

The Reverend Dr Alexander Whyte bought the house in 1889. Whyte was born to a single mother in Kirriemuir and served an apprenticeship to a shoemaker before becoming a schoolteacher. He saved up enough money to attend Aberdeen University and then New College, Edinburgh, to study divinity. From 1870 to 1896 he was minister of Free St George's Church in nearby Shandwick Place, and in 1898 he became the Moderator of the Free Church of Scotland General Assembly. He was known as a powerful preacher. He married Jane Barbour of Bonskeid in 1880, and the couple had eight children, one of whom, Robert, was killed in action aged 24 in the First World War. Jane continued to live in the house after her husband's death in 1921.

This portrait of Lord Neaves appeared in the Glasgow journal, The Bailie, *in 1875*

One of the Whytes' sons, Lancelot, vividly described life at No. 7, where the family used the rooms very differently from their predecessors: 'On the [second] floor I only remember two bedrooms: my father's small room, which did not count, and my mother's, which most decidedly did. For it was big and full of strange objects, scents, and other mysteries … my mother sitting up in bed writing letters to extraordinary men all over the world: men with dreams to convert mankind … to new and better religions and more wonderful ways of living … One floor further down was my father's enormous study, a room of dignity with 6,000 books, where he would be writing sermons or letters to simple unhappy men and women everywhere … On the ground floor was a large schoolroom … devoted to "muscular Christianity", for it was turned into a gymnasium, complete with parallel bars.' The son of the founder of the Baha'i faith, Abdu'l-Baha, stayed in the house as a guest of the Whytes during an official trip to Edinburgh in January 1913. A plaque on the second floor commemorates his visit.

The 4th Marquess of Bute (1881–1947) bought No. 7 in 1927, adding to his previous purchases of Nos. 5 and 6. Inspired by the Adam Revival of the late 19th century and driven by a passionate

Dr Alexander Whyte

The dining room at No. 7 in use as an office for Whytock & Reid

interest in townscape, he removed the Victorian alterations to the north side of the Square and did much to restore the original appearance of Adam's 'palace front'. In 1934 Bute leased the house to Whytock & Reid, Edinburgh's leading cabinetmakers and upholsterers.

After the 5th Marquess of Bute's death in 1956, No. 7, along with Nos. 5 and 6 Charlotte Square, passed to the National Trust for Scotland as part fulfilment of death duties. The transfer, through National Land Fund procedures, was completed in 1966. To comply with the wishes of the 6th Marquess, who stipulated that the buildings should remain a 'home', the Trust agreed to No. 6 becoming the official residence of the Secretary of State for Scotland and, after devolution, of the First Minister of Scotland.

Whytock & Reid continued to lease No. 7 until 1973, when the Trust began work on the basement, ground floor and first floor to turn them into a typical Georgian town house. In August 1975 the house was opened to the public, furnished and arranged as it might have been by its first occupants, the Lamont family. The Trust then modified the top two floors with the help of the Baird Trust in order to let them as the official residence of the Moderator of the General Assembly of the Church of Scotland. This arrangement continued until 1999, since when the second floor has been used for educational visits and Trust meetings.

The 4th Marquess of Bute

Re-creating Adam's vision

This photograph from the early 1900s shows the north side of the Square before Lord Bute's restoration

The appearance of the north side of Charlotte Square today reflects Adam's original intentions so closely that it is difficult to appreciate how much fashionable alteration was made during the late 19th century in the name of giving individual character to each house, but damaging Adam's vision of the unified whole. The Victorian aesthetic was best expressed by John Ruskin in his Edinburgh lectures of 1853: 'Walk round Edinburgh buildings, and look at the height of your eye … Nothing but square-cut stone … a wilderness of square-cut stone for ever and ever; so that your houses look like prisons.' Lord Neaves at No. 7 was one of those householders who thought that 'the proposed alterations will be beneficial to … the property'.

The 4th Marquess of Bute bought No. 5 Charlotte Square in 1903, possibly to stave off a planning threat. His father, the 3rd Marquess, a great patron of the arts and restorer of Falkland Palace, had encouraged him to take a close interest in historic buildings – and if possible to intervene where they were threatened. Bute's subsequent purchase of Nos. 6 and 7 gave him possession of the vital centrepiece of the palace front on the north side, and an interest in the future of the entire Square. Externally, he removed dormer windows (including those added to No. 7 by the Whytes), increased the height of the drawing room windows, restored astragals to windows that had been fitted with plate glass, and put back fanlights over doors.

Inside, Bute was no less thorough. By 1915 No. 5 was being held up as a model of classical elegance, in contrast to its neighbours. In 1927, Bute began on the interior of No. 7, restoring the proportions of the original Drawing Room (used as a study by the Reverend Whyte) and – in a misplaced excess of zeal – removing the original Georgian sideboard recesses in the two ground-floor rooms.

Bute's restoration work was recognised when, in 1930, the City of Edinburgh Council brought in the Edinburgh Town Planning (Charlotte Square) Scheme order, protecting Adam's architectural vision for the future.

No. 7 in the care of the Trust

Due to Charlotte Square's status as a fashionable address, the houses were often altered to suit changing tastes. No. 7 had been extensively redecorated for the Rev. Dr Whyte by the architectural decorators Scott Morton & Co, and the stone stair had been given a timber balustrade and casing.

When the Trust decided to open the property to the public, a committee was established to supervise the re-creation of a Georgian House at No. 7 and visited the then-existing sister Georgian Houses in Bristol and Bath. The Trust had to undertake some changes, principally the new cornices and door surrounds in the Drawing Room, newly designed by the architect Schomberg Scott.

It was seen as crucial to conceal the servicing of the house and thus the heating is by way of ducts with grilles in the floor. Lighting was concealed on the tops of tall furniture like the curtain boxes and the bookcase in the Parlour.

Restoration work on the frieze in the Parlour

The chimneypiece in the front drawing room was vandalised during the Trust's restoration of the house and was replaced by one from the bedroom floor of No. 5, almost certainly introduced there by the 4th Marquess of Bute.

Although paint investigation was carried out in this much altered house, the Trust was guided by the paint investigation concurrently being carried out at Adam's near-contemporary Culzean Castle in Ayrshire.

The creation of a Georgian Kitchen by the Trust's Curator David Learmont was highly innovative and led to a renewed interest in historic kitchens and their restoration in many country houses. David Learmont also built up a fine collection of Sheffield plate for display in the Dining Room.

Restoration work in the Drawing Room

It was not easy to establish instantly an appropriate collection to dress the house and the house relied on generous gifts and loans, with some items being borrowed from other Trust properties. From the outset, the Georgian House benefited from an outstanding loan of paintings from the Wayne family. The Trust already had the fine suite of painted and gilded sofa and chairs from Yester House, East Lothian. An oval Adam-style pier glass from Leith Hall was copied to create a pair for the Drawing Room piers. The three curtain cornices in the Drawing Room, made by John Linnel for Croome Court in Worcestershire, were donated by John Partridge (Fine Arts) Ltd, London. The most spectacular loan was the late 18th-century bed with appliqué needlework hangings, lent from Newliston House, West Lothian, but subsequently purchased by the Trust with the assistance of a grant from the National Art Fund. It has always been intended to showcase items with a Scottish provenance, like the Bruce & Burns tea table in the Parlour and the square piano in the Drawing Room.

Many items have become more interesting because of their donors, like the decorative painting over the chimneypiece in the Bedchamber donated by the late Eleanor Robertson, who founded the Scottish Georgian Society that campaigned to save George Square.

Gladstone's Land

A six-storey tenement on Edinburgh's Royal Mile that dates from the 17th century. Thomas Gledstanes, a wealthy merchant, owned the 'land'; he may have occupied the third floor with his family and rented out the other floors to tenants of various means. By the 18th century, the cramped conditions of living in this kind of tenement was one of the catalysts that brought about the desire to create the New Town. Six display rooms have been furnished with objects of the period, invoking how life might have been in the Old Town 400 years ago.

Directions: on the Lawnmarket, at the top end of the Royal Mile

Open: Easter to October, 10–5 (6.30 during July and August), daily
Tel: 0844 493 2120

Distance: 1 mile from the Georgian House

Newhailes

Sir David Dalrymple, Lord Advocate and Solicitor-General for Scotland, built what was probably the largest private library of its time in Scotland at Newhailes in 1718. It is easy to imagine key figures of the Enlightenment gathered in this room for discussion and debate surrounded by Dalrymple's vast collection of books. Dr Johnson reportedly described the library as 'the most learned drawing room in Europe'. This dignified 17th-century home, with 18th-century additions, has not been restored to an immaculate dwelling; instead, the Trust has worked hard to keep the house 'untouched' by modern hands.

Directions: on Newhailes Road (A6095) in Musselburgh

Open: Easter to September (please check website for opening times)
Tel: 0844 493 2125

Distance: 6½ miles from the Georgian House (good bus links from Edinburgh city centre)

Edinburgh

The Georgian House

Gladstone's Land

Newhailes

A1

A7

A772